Bingley History Trail

by

Gary Firth

For Rachel and Asa

Published by Hendon Publishing Company Limited, Hendon Mill, Nelson, Lancashire.
Text © Gary Firth, 1977
Printed by: Fretwell & Brian Ltd., Howden Hall, Silsden, Keighley, Yorks.

History Trail of Bingley

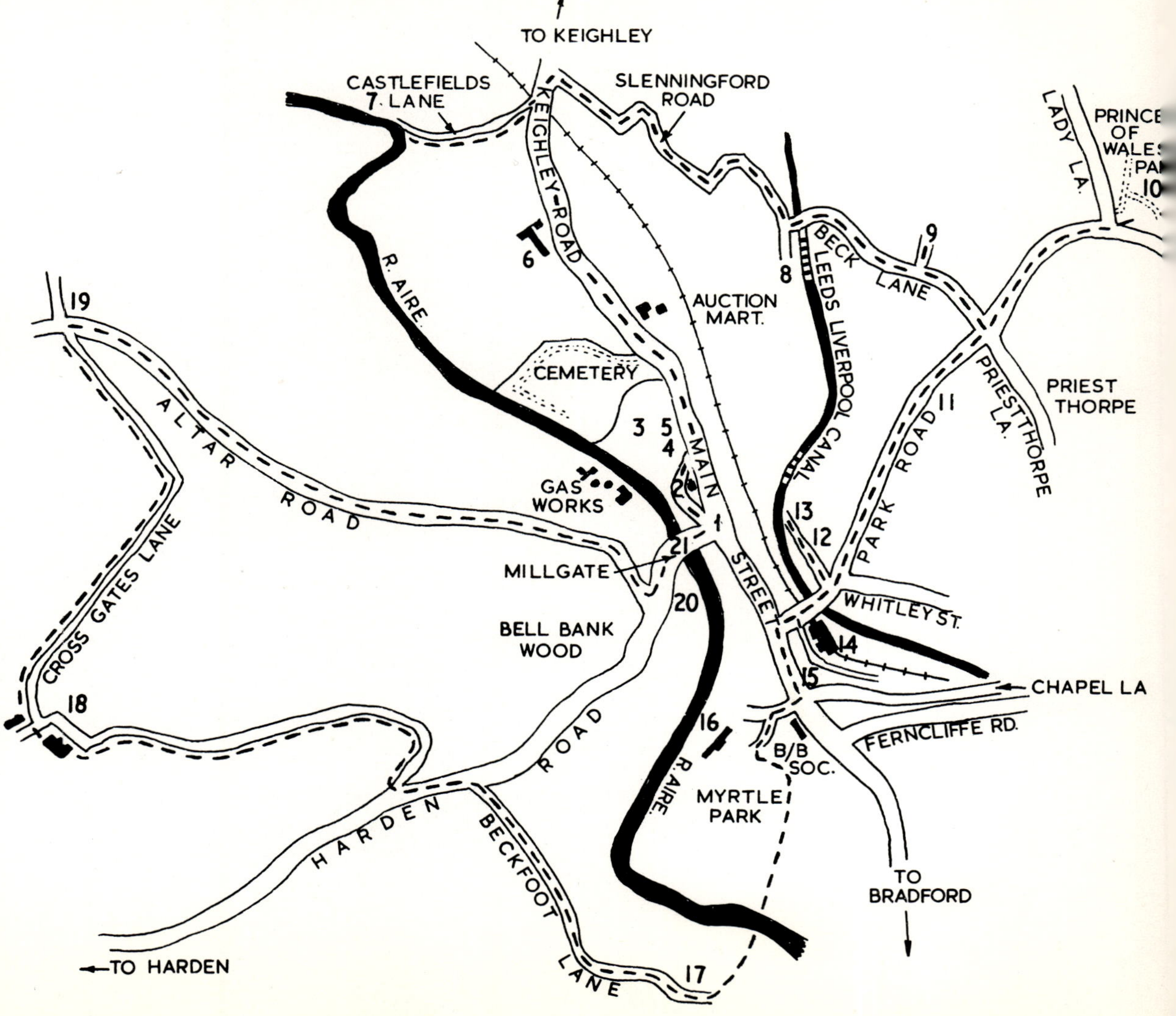

Key:

Trail - - - -

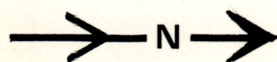

→→ N →

TO KEIGHLEY

CASTLEFIELDS 7 LANE

SLENNINGFORD ROAD

KEIGHLEY ROAD

R. AIRE

6

AUCTION MART.

CEMETERY

8

BECK LANE

9

LEEDS LIVERPOOL CANAL

LADY LA.

PRINCE OF WALES PARK

10

19

ALTAR ROAD

3 5 4

MAIN STREET

GAS WORKS

13

12

PARK ROAD 11

PRIESTTHORPE LA.

PRIEST THORPE

CROSS GATES LANE

MILLGATE

21

1

20

WHITLEY ST.

BELL BANK WOOD

14

15

CHAPEL LA.

18

HARDEN ROAD

BECKFOOT LANE

16

B/B SOC.

FERNCLIFFE RD.

R. AIRE

MYRTLE PARK

TO BRADFORD

←TO HARDEN

17

Introduction

George Canning, a 19th century statesman and former Prime Minister once remarked "I called the New World into existence to redress the balance of the Old". Such has been the work of local and central government in the past few years in Bingley. Much to the regret of certain members of the community, a new Bingley will emerge from the recent surge of redevelopment. The shopping arcade, arts centre, multi-storey office block and high rise flats are all part and parcel of the effort to forge a new image.

It is, however, essential to preserve the historical heritage of the town. This booklet is an attempt to do just that. The selected items which follow hopefully paint a fragmentary yet realistic picture of the historical development of Bingley. The ancient parish church as it nestles beneath the legendary Bailey Hills; Old Main Street, the town centre of a bygone age; the mills and canals to remind us of the industrial and technological world we have inherited; all these have played their part in the drama of Bingley's growth.

Perhaps as you make your way along ancient highways and wander into hidden corners, you might let your imagination conjure up the mystical Druid, the Saxon serf, the clash of Royalist and Roundhead, Wesley in the churchyard and even an English Prime Minister playing cricket at Cottingley Bridge.

This guide will lead you step by step around the trail, though this need not be religiously followed. Our trail starts at the lower end of the town at the junction of Millgate and . . .

The map on the facing page is for your guidance as you follow the trail. It shows the location of the outlying points of interest as well as those close to the centre of the town.

OLD MAIN STREET (1)

By far the most picturesque part of old Bingley, this highway (the subject of our cover picture) is also the oldest part of the town for it is the ancient highway along the valley, the path of Celtic tribes. Today it boasts a collection of miscellaneous housing styles ranging over four centuries.

At the junction of Old Main Street and Millgate stands the Old White Horse Inn. It was from the mounting steps of this old coaching inn that John Wesley preached to a congregation too large to be housed in the Parish Church. Wesley made thirteen visits to Bingley with "so genteel a congregation; yet the word of God fell heavily upon them". The inn was one of the town's three coaching inns, as one can see from the adjoining livery stables and courtyard to the rear. Note also the stone lanterns at the gable corners, said to be an ownership symbol of the Knights of St. John of Jerusalem.

Opposite the Old White Horse Inn on the other side of Millgate are a number of very old cottages which adjoined the ancient Corn Mill. The site of this ancient mill is now occupied by Hempel's whose building itself is the 18th century corn mill of the town with its own mill goit. In the 13th century the value of the soke mill was one third the value of the whole manor!

Standing opposite the main entrance to the church is Church House. This is an old building though formerly it served a less reverend purpose. Before 1928 it was the Ring O' Bells public house where boats could be hired in summer time for those lazy trips up the river towards Marley. Close to Church House is a large cottage which has a date stone of 1770, a period of great building enterprise in this part of the world.

Many of these cottages were formerly shops. Today's houses are single residences from several old cottages.

The Old Main Street of today is only the remains of a much larger highway stretching right through the town. The transition to industry brought full urbanisation and the town expanded rapidly in the mid 19th century. The urban structure of the town was changed drastically in 1882 when the Improvement Commission purchased the manorial rights and various Main Street plots. In 1904 the main highway was straightened when a road was cut through the graveyard. This made obsolete the present Old Main Street, which remains today a fine testimony of a Bingley that has long since passed away.

Moving along Old Main Street you will note how this old cobbled highway is dominated by the fine . . .

PARISH CHURCH (ALL SAINTS) (2)

In the reconstruction work of 1870/71 the fragment of a Saxon cross was found on this site. It is quite possible, therefore, that there was a pre Norman church here. The church that was built in the Norman period was not small, for several sizeable capitals and pillars were found in 1870. The church was given to the Augustinian order at Drax Priory by William Pagnel, Lord of the Manor. That order provided a priest from 1197 until the dissolution of 1536.

The greater part of the present church is sixteenth century. The choir was built in 1518 by Rev. Richard Wylson, Prior of Drax and a native of the town. The short 15th century tower was extended in 1739. Inside the church, the Perpendicular

See p. 32 &

style is apparent in the lower chancel where there are five bays with slender octagonal piers. Above can be seen the straight-headed triple windows of the clerestory. There is no triforium.

A west gallery and heavy wooded organ loft were removed in the reconstruction of 1870/1. At a cost of £3,000 the re-structuring thus opened the tower arch to the nave, and the Ryshworth Chapel was added on the north side.

RELICS.

There is a small collection of early 18th century silver plate, including two chalices and a flagon. There is some fine heraldic glass in the West window of the tower (local gentry) and an excellent show of 16th century glass in the East window of the Riddlesden Chapel. The parish registers date from 1577 and are in excellent condition, though they are now in the care of Bradford Central Library. Perhaps the most famous of the relics is the Runic Stone (at the west end of the nave). The Stone is square and is clearly inscribed, although authorities have disputed the translation of the inscription. Its date and purpose can only be guessed at, though it would appear characteristic of the Late Saxon-Early Norman period.

THE GRAVEYARD.

The parish graveyard is to be found around the church and across the main road. Formerly the north side housed those who had received the poor relief. There were some interesting stones, but many were lost or removed in the road construction of 1904, including that of John Nicholson, poet of Airedale. One gravestone on the north side of the church records that, William Shaw sober laborious & faithfull Who at 2s per Week for above 40 years in one family maintained a Wife and numerous Issue.

The old graveyard was inadequate by the mid 19th century and in 1869 land was purchased on Bailey Hills for £9,000. It was officially opened in 1871. Now make your way up the gently sloping road opposite the church tower and you will reach . . .

BAILEY HILLS (3)

Early local historians have argued strongly that this was the site of the original "Bingley", the Celtic settlement. Certainly there was no fortification built on this site after the Norman invasion and what Dodsworth referred to as a "castle" in the 16th century was perhaps little more than tradition and legend. However, the site is naturally suited to early habitation.

With the floods of the post Ice-Age period Bailey Hills was made an island with a glacial lake to the north ('Bingley Bog') and a steeply wooded riverbank to the south. Where the island tapers to an apex at Ireland Bridge, there is Belbank Wood, "bel" being the Gaelic for ford or entrance. For further substantiation of this argument, H. Speight's "Old Bingley" should be consulted. Returning the way you came, drop back into Old Main Street and turn left towards the main Keighley road. Passing some delightful old cottages you will come to the substantial . . .

SCHOOLMASTER'S HOUSE (4)

Formerly the site of the ancient Newhall, this fine building

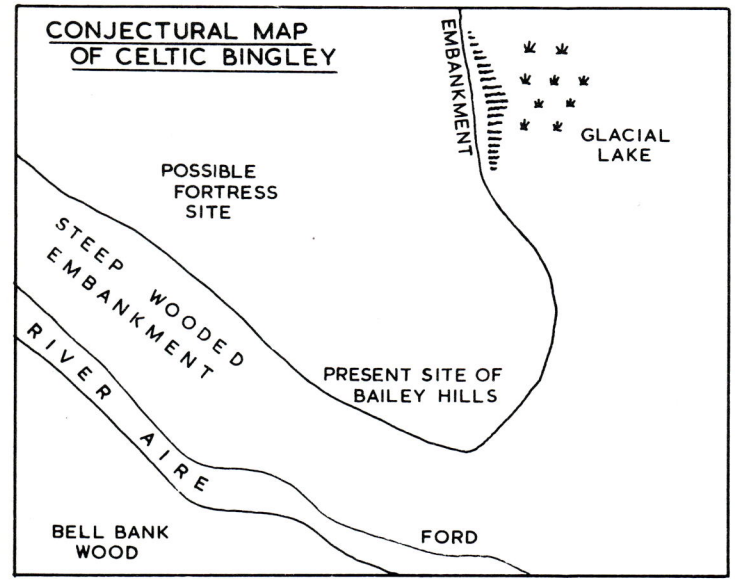

CONJECTURAL MAP OF CELTIC BINGLEY

EMBANKMENT

GLACIAL LAKE

POSSIBLE FORTRESS SITE

STEEP WOODED EMBANKMENT

RIVER AIRE

PRESENT SITE OF BAILEY HILLS

BELL BANK WOOD

FORD

A programme of repairs was undertaken in 1676 and the house was leased to the highest bidder. It is doubtful whether schoolmasters occupied the building in the 17th century. That practice commenced in 1746 with the appointment of Thomas Hudson, a former master at the Otley and Hipperholme schools. Hudson brought six pupils from the latter school and these boys were boarded in the house. After Hudson's death (1756) the number of boarders increased quite considerably. Under the headmastership of Dr. Richard Hartley (vicar 1797/1837) extensive repairs and improvements were undertaken. In 1797/8 he spent £450 on "Newhall" so that by 1816 it could house 36 boarders from the school. It remained the official residence of the vicar of Bingley in the years 1837/51 when the practice was finally described as "a gross act of trespass".

By now the annual value of the property was £20 p.a. and in 1851 it became the schoolmaster's house once more. In 1853 the school left its ancient site alongside the parish church and moved to the site of the present Auction Mart. The upheavals in the national education movement after 1870 took effect on the Bingley Grammar School. Newhall was to be converted into cottages, but this proposal was abandoned and the governors of the school finally sold the property to Mr. Philip Astley for £525. Its sale broke a great tradition, for after three hundred years there was no schoolmaster's house!

does much to preserve the character of "old Bingley". Its condition is a tribute to the governors of the Grammar School and to its more recent owners. It is believed that the house stands upon the site of Newhall, an ancient dwelling of the medieval manor of Bingley.

Certainly by 1571 the Newhall was worth only 8/– per year and by 1601, when John Milner leased it as a schoolmaster's house, its value had slipped to 5/– p.a. Its value had increased fourfold by 1635, but forty years later it was described by a contemporary as "ruinous and sore out of repair"!

Overleaf: Schoolmaster's House, Main Street.

Almost adjoining Newhall and facing the main Bradford-Keighley road is a row of three storeyed buildings, the so called . . .

WEAVERS' COTTAGES (5)

A three hundred yard walk along the main highway towards Keighley will take you past the town's cemetery on the left and the Auction Mart on the right, and will eventually bring you to . . .

THE GRAMMAR SCHOOL (6)

There has been an institution for the teaching of grammar at Bingley for almost four hundred and fifty years. In 1529 an endowment was made of lands at Greenhill to provide for a master to teach grammar in the town. The present school functions on the 'house' basis, and each of the four houses takes the name of an early benefactor to the school. One of these, William Wooller, a wealthy Merchant Adventurer of the late Elizabethan period left several landed estates to the school in his will of 1597.

A century later Samuel Sunderland, a Halifax merchant and benefactor to several local schools, gave lands in Heaton and Wilsden. On his death Sunderland left a fortune of £17,000 and land which provided an annual income of £1,200. In subsequent years there were other small bequests made to the governors of the school. The first school was built between the years 1637 and 1667 on a site now occupied by the main road, alongside the Parish Church and opposite the White Horse Inn. However, the educational needs of an expanding 19th century town like Bingley rendered this building obsolete (it was demolished in 1904).

Bingley Grammar School, 1853

The present BINGLEY GRAMMAR SCHOOL is a succession of extensions to an original building which was transferred from another site. In 1853 the new grammar school was constructed on land which now houses the Bingley Auction Market. Costing £1,000, this building was declared unsafe by a government inspector in October 1860. The "Bingley Bog" on which it had been erected soon caused structural distortions and the school was actually rebuilt on the present site, in Little Castlefield. The original school is the present Dining Hall of the Bingley Grammar School, and although completed in 1863, it carries the date stone of the original building. As the educational system expanded in the latter part of the 19th century, so did the educational facilities at the school.

Expansion meant the need for new buildings. These were commenced in 1906 and completed in the following year. They are the present 'A' block and today form the main entrance to the school. This new complex was used as the Boys' Grammar School. The girls of Bingley moved into the older block. A wall separated the two schools.

The inadequacy of the 1907 building was soon apparent. With the aid of a County Council grant the governors of the school commenced a scheme of some stature. A very long extension was added to the 1907 building, thus forming a T-shape. The drainage of the land caused building problems, but the ambitious project was completed in 1931. This new extension housed the Girls' Grammar School, while the boys remained in the lower buildings.

The trail now continues along the A650 heading for Keighley. Shortly before this road crosses the railway at Crossflatts, there is Castlefield Lane leading off to the left. At the bottom of this Lane will be found the . . .

CASTLEFIELD MILL (7)

Beyond the main gate of the mill is private property and permission should be sought for a detailed investigation of the site.

The mill at Castlefields, Bingley, was commenced in 1792, when a group of local merchants and gentlemen formed a partnership to produce cotton yarn on a large scale. The group included James Sidgwick, Wilmer Mackett Willett, Joseph Wood and the local squire, J. A. Busfeild. On 26th December, 1793, Wood and Sidgwick dropped out of the partnership. Young women and children were employed at the few spinning machines which had been installed, but in time a large trade was built up. Busfeild sold his cotton twist in Blackburn market and probably returned from there with packs of cotton from his workers, at "the Shop" as he called it. The mill was valued at £7,000, which was quite considerable for that time.

By 1805 the mill had passed into the hands of Mr. Lister Ellis from Bolton in Lancs. His trade must have been good for we know that he was the first factory owner in Yorkshire to instal gas lighting in his mill. He also rebuilt Castlefields House for himself and his family.

However, the mill continued to be driven by a 40 h.p. water wheel which was powered by a goit running from the river Aire, alongside the mill. In March 1823 the mill at Castlefields employed 112 persons, of which only 24 were male. They included whole families like the Wild's, Baldwin, Lister, Whaley, Rhodes, Walbank and Butterfield. Several of these families lived in the Crossflatts cottages about 500 yards from

the mill, or in the Castlefields Cottages (built in 1825 and only recently demolished). Other workers came to the mill from the hamlets of Crow Nest, Marley, Gilstead and Eldwick.

Ten years later in 1833 there were 130 persons employed at the mill, of which 109 were women (19 were under 14 years old). However, "the age affords no criterion of the wages paid: ability is the principal test". By this time Lister Ellis had passed on the mill to his son William whose employees worked from six o'clock in the morning until seven thirty at night, with an hour for lunch. Ellis gave his workers $7\frac{1}{2}$ days holiday each year and fined them for lateness and bad work. He refused to use corporal punishment.

The factory workers at Castlefields were more fortunate than most, for when sickness kep them from work, their master provided half-pay for three consecutive weeks. However, this was not as generous as it first appeared for most of the sick pay came from "a sick fund raised by a general contribution of the workpeople by a weekly rate, and something is added by the proprietor of the mill". As factory masters went, William Ellis was probably one of the better sort. He was co-founder and manager of the Bingley National school; he opposed the Poor Law of 1834 in the interests of local workers and was an able magistrate until his death in 1856. However, in the early 1830's he had little sympathy for Oastler's Ten Hour Movement. He believed such a short day ridiculous, making it impossible for English cotton masters to compete with the French who were spinning until ten o'clock at night.

This, therefore, is a brief description of an early factory at Bingley. Like thousands of others in the industrial North, the pay was low, the hours long, the conditions were poor and it was quite normal to employ children under the age of seven.

Yet this was one of the better mills and its proprietor one of the more enlightened of factory masters!

Returning to the Keighley highway you cross to the other side. Children take extra care, it is a very busy road! You will come to Slenningford Road which will lead you (after a short walk) to the towpath of the Leeds-Liverpool Canal. Follow your map closely at this point. On reaching the towpath make your way back into Bingley and after a hundred yards or so you will reach a swing bridge which overlooks the world famous . . .

FIVE RISE LOCKS (8)

The Five Rise Locks on the Leeds-Liverpool Canal at Bingley are often quoted as one of the wonders of the early industrial world. The coming of the canal age marked the end of Bingley as a rural backwater. For the town was then placed upon one of the main arteries of 18th century trade and commerce. As early as 1744 there had been a project to navigate the River Aire from Cottingley to Inghay Bridge at Skipton, but this did not materialise. The activity of a group of Bradford men in the late 1760's, to promote a canal from Leeds to Liverpool, had more success. Thanks largely to the efforts of John Stanhope and, more important, John Hustler, a Bradford merchant and Quaker, an act of parliament was passed for such a waterway in 1770.

The route chosen by the surveyor and engineer, John Longbotham, included the Aire valley from Skipton to Leeds. However, the scheme was delayed temporarily when a group of Bingley landlords demanded unrealistic prices for land through which the canal was to pass. Benjamin Ferrand, Miles Staveley and the Trustees of Bingley Grammar School were holding out for £160 per acre. A meeting was held, at the Elm Tree Inn, Bingley, 20th March, 1771, of the canal com-missioners, but they included Ferrand and Staveley! The matter was decided at the crowded Bingley Methodist Church by a jury which awarded the landowners £80 per acre on a compulsory purchase system.

Eventually work began on the stretch of the canal from Skipton to Shipley. The Five Rise and Three Rise Locks were engineered by Longbotham, but constructed by masons from Bingley and Wilsden. The Thackley-Skipton stretch of the canal was finally opened 21st March, 1774; the first boat down the Five Rise Locks taking 28 minutes. The event was given full coverage in the "Leeds Intelligencer".

"From Bingley to about 3 miles downwards the noblest works of the kind . . . are exhibited viz:- A fivefold, a threefold, a twofold and a single lock, making together a fall of 120 feet; a large aqueduct bridge of seven arches over the River Aire and an aqueduct and banking over the Shipley valley . . . This joyful and much wished for event was welcomed with the ringing of Bingley bells, a band of music, the firing of guns by the neighbouring Militia, the shouts of the spectators, and all the marks of satisfaction that so important an acquisition merits".

Adjoining the swing-bridge is the original lock-keeper's cottage, and although not in much demand these days from commercial traffic, the lock-keeper is kept busy in the summer months, for this is a popular stretch of water with pleasure boat owners.

Overleaf: Five Rise Locks, Bingley.

13

Cross the swing bridge at the top of the locks and bear right into Beck Lane. Before reaching the junction with Hall Bank Drive, there is a narrow road to the left which climbs the hill and leads to the private residence of . . .

GAWTHORPE HALL (9)

This fine hall is supposed to have been built in the last decade of the 16th century. It was bought by one, Anthony Walker, in 1596 as part of the manor lord's property, although it was not recognised as the manor house. Speight suggests that it was probably part of an older building owned by the priory at Drax.

Much of the present building suffered serious alteration under John Horsfall who purchased the estate from the Lane-Fox family in 1854. It was originally of an E-shape, but the two recesses were filled out to give the effect of a full front. The gables have mullioned and transomed windows of five to seven bays. The hall is now divided into a number of luxury flats and the interior is consequently much changed by structural and decorative alterations.

Perhaps the Hall's most celebrated occupant was Robert Benson, whose father bought the estate from Henry Currer in 1668. Benson Jnr. became M.P. for York and later Chancellor of the Exchequer. He was made Lord Bingley in 1713, though his title was only a life peerage and thus died with him in 1731. Having established his fortune and reputation, Benson spent little of his time at Gawthorpe, preferring London and Bramham Hall, which he built.

Gawthorpe Hall.

Retracing your steps to Beck Lane, pass up Gawthorpe Lane and turn right into Spa Lane, location of the ancient pinfold. Once in Park Road walk up the hill to the entrance of the Prince of Wales Park (opened 1865) and within the grounds you will be signposted to the . . .

MARKET CROSS & STOCKS (10)

There has recently been a move to bring the market cross and stocks from the Prince of Wales Park to a more appropriate focal point in Main Street. If it succeeds, this will reverse the decisions of the town council of 1888 when the Market Hall stood opposite Ferrand Lane, so splicing the main highway.

Overleaf: Market Hall and Cross.

15

The Heart of Old Bingley...

Bingley 'Tide',
Main Street, 1904

Left: Chapel Lane in the 1880's, showing the old Independent Chapel.   Below: Bingley Market Place removed to Prince of Wales Park in 1888.

Main Street again, this time around 1900, showing the original line of the highway.

—continued from page 16

Bingley was first granted its market charter by King John in 1212. Farmers from the outlying hamlets brought in their goods each Sunday and probably traded in the precinct of the church. Such a practice was abolished by a statute of 1284. Over the centuries market day changed from Monday to Thursday, and later to Tuesday. In addition Bingley was allowed to hold two fairs each year. The market cross was probably placed at the top of Ferrand Lane. However, the vestry officials of the mid 18th century determined on an ambitious scheme of a market hall and new Butter Cross.

This was completed in 1753 by Thomas Lister, "at the considerable expense" of £12.13.10½. The building in the park is the same, with slight alterations. In spite of such facilities, and a directive from leading tradesmen "That we will not buy or sell any butter, eggs, fowl, ducks, geese, turkeys, pidgeons, potatoes, apples, onions or other vegetables (pease only excepted) otherwise than in the Public Market", the trade done at the Bingley market continued to decline. When an outbreak of Black Plague occurred in the town in 1787, many tradesmen went to Otley market and never returned.

THE STOCKS

The public punishment for crimes and criminals of a trivial nature. The target for small boys with rotten vegetables; the criminal more often suffered ridicule and humiliation than physical pain. The stocks at Bingley are said to have been the last in use in Yorkshire; 1870 is given as the date. Certainly they were still employed in 1866.

On leaving the Prince of Wales Park by the Lady Lane exit make your way back into the town via Park Road until you reach the junction with Priestthorpe Lane. Here is the site of the ancient hamlet of Priestthorpe worked from the waste lands in the 12th century. Below Priestthorpe Lane on the left is a substantial building which backs onto Park Road; this is . . .

MONK BARN (11)

The building which goes by this name is the Old Vicarage, although it has not been used for that purpose since the early 17th century. This area, known as Priestthorpe, formerly belonged to the Augustinian Priory at Drax, in the former East Riding. The monks built a house inhabited by Bingley's vicars of the middle ages, but during the Dissolution the estate passed to the Paslew family. Thomas Cromwell confirmed this tenure on condition that a great tithe barn was erected. Each year the Church received one tenth ("tythe") of the individual's income from the land, either in goods or money.

The barn was built and did not disappear until 1910. The vicarage itself, which had taken the name of Monk Barn, was constructed in the early 17th century. Its L-shape has a projecting gable and much of the south front was altered in the latter part of the 18th century. It is a private house and permission for a more detailed scrutiny of the building should be obtained from the proprietors.

Dropping further into the town centre, via Park Road, you will now pass some fine terrace houses of the late Victorian period, and occasional detached residences of some size from the same period. Shortly before the bridge, over the railway, on the righthand side is the . . .

NATIONAL SCHOOL (12)

In an age when school buildings are of doubtful architectural quality and permanence, this small school is a quiet testimony to the builders and educational pioneers in the days before Waterloo! As early as 1784, John Wesley in his journal referred to the Bingley Sunday School "containing 240 children taught by several masters and superintended by the curate". Shared by Anglicans and Dissenters, such a school catered in its own way for the needs of Bingley's poorer children. However, doctrinal differences and the need for a more secular education, caused the denominations to go their own ways.

As the inscription shows, this building is one of the earliest examples in the North of the National School system, an Anglican organisation promoting schools on the monitorial lines laid down by Rev. Andrew Bell. Erected in 1814, on land owned by the Ferrand family, it cost £1,600, of which £300 was given by the London National School Society. The remainder came from a local subscription, to which all leading dignitaries contributed. A committee, including General Twiss, Reverend Hartley, Edward Ferrand and William Ellis of Castlefields, managed the affairs of the school. However, in April, 1821, the committee appointed William Hepworth as master of the school. He made his own charges and paid his own expenses (except fuel). The Girls' School flourished, there being 90 pupils in 1823. However, there were only half that number of boys (there had been 106 boys in 1817). The following is an extract from a letter from the master of the school to the trustees: "The Bingley Girls' National School is well conducted and answers a useful purpose, the Boys' School exists, but is in a very languishing state, the middling and lower classes of persons in this country being chiefly

Methodists or Dissenters have a great dislike to the National System of Education—added to this our population is chiefly manufacturing and the boys can earn money for their parents at so early a period of life that they are not disposed to forego the advantages desired from the labour of their children. The Master Manufacturers being chiefly Methodists will not, I believe, employ any children but such as attend their Sunday School . . .all this materially affects the Bingley National School".

National School, Lime Street.

The result was that the school was temporarily closed when Hepworth left in 1824. Six years later the Girls' School met a similar fate. A clause in the 1833 Factory Act compelled children in mills to receive two hours education each day. This revived the National School at Bingley which became one of the town's five factory schools. Peel's Factory Act commenced the "half-time" system which lasted well into the 20th century.

The National School figured in Bingley's worst disaster in 1869 when a boiler, adjoining the school yard, exploded and killed 15 persons, including several children playing in the school yard at the time. The school faces . . .

LIME STREET (13)

There is little here now, apart from the street name, to remind us of an industry once flourishing in Bingley. Skipton was the main centre of limestone burning, but during the glacial movements of the Ice Age pockets of limestone were brought down from Craven and were deposited in the Bingley area.

The earliest lime-burning kilns in Bingley were to be found in the present Myrtle Park and were close to the quarry where the limestone was found, crushed and then burnt. The kilns were simple square "pye-kilns" and were filled with alternate layers of limestone and coal (or charcoal). There was also a "drawing kiln" from which the bottom layer was removed as another layer was added at the top. This allowed the kiln to be used continuously.

The flourishing state of the trade was boosted by the great building boom of the second half of the 18th century. Thus a person at the time could say:

"It appears by the accounts of the two chief dealers in Lyme at Bingley, that they formerly have sold and delivered near 40,000 horse loads of lime yearly, but that at present (through the scarcity of limestone) they do not deliver much above half that quantity. That they sell lime at Bingley two bushels at 9 pence and say that if they had limestone enough to burn, they would sell a great deal more lime than they do now".

At the same time as using its own natural limestone, Bingley developed an important entrepot trade with Skipton. Limestone was brought down from Skipton and processed in the Bingley kilns. In return the Skipton farmers and tradesmen took back supplies of coal from pits around East Morton and more important from those at Bradford belonging to men like Edward Leedes, John Jarratt, and John Hustler. In those days coal was brought by horse on the Bradford-Haworth road and then down to Cottingley Bar. From there it came along the main road into Bingley i.e. along Beckfoot Lane. Such a route was slow, costly and hindered trade; a new means of transport was desirable.

In 1770 the work on the Leeds-Liverpool canal was commenced and by April 1774 the stretch from Skipton to Shipley was completed. Consequently the lime burning trade expanded, as John Hustler remarked in a letter to the press. The following is taken from the Leeds Intelligencer, 28th June 1774:

"On the Yorkshire side we found 18 boats of burthen already built, a number of which have been for some time fully employed between Skipton and Bingley, in the lime and coal trade. There are forty lime-kilns now erected and preparing between Skipton and Bradford; and

the demand for lime is so great that the business on the line in this article and in coals must be soon very large."

The main quarrying centres in Bingley were situated at the end of Beckfoot Lane (now the golf course); the end of the present Southlands Grove in what was then known as Myrtle Pasture; and finally a site in Prince of Wales Park was an old limestone quarry. The limestone was burned in a number of kilns situated directly in front of the National School and adjoining the canal. Thus, the origin of Lime Street is explained.

Left: Cottingley Toll Bar, now demolished.

At the very end of Park Road, on the left, is Wellington Street which provides the forecourt of . . .

THE RAILWAY AT BINGLEY (14)

The railway age is said to have been the second industrial revolution. Bingley was first placed upon the railway map in 1846/7. In the first of these years a line had been completed from Leeds to Bradford. It was the Leeds & Bradford Railway Company which decided to run a line to Colne via Skipton and the Aire Gap. Tenders were issued and Messrs. George Thompson & Company were contracted to build the line from Keighley to the Shipley Junction. The line included such difficulties as the Bingley tunnel and the river bridge at Dowley Gap, but by far the most formidable of tasks was the crossing of the infamous Bingley Bog. This was overcome by depositing over 100,000 cubic yards of stone and earth into the marshy land.

The line was finished by the spring of 1847 and had taken only nine months to complete. An experimental run, taking local dignatories along the line, took place on 1st March. The

engine "Camilla" and three coaches (all draped in Union Jacks!) stopped at Bingley before an excited crowd of 3,000. During the official speech, "a female navvy, cleanly attired, her bonnet be-decked with ribbons . . . hurra'd lustily". As the day had been declared a general holiday, no doubt this young lady had imbibed freely from the 36 gallons of ale given to the construction gangs!

A fortnight later the line was open to the public; eight trains running in each direction daily. Hundreds of Bradford mill girls had saved for the sixpenny ride to Keighley, but unable to afford a return fare, walked the journey home.

The first Bingley station was situated in Dean's Yard (near the present station on Park Road corner). The second re-siting took place in July 1892, when the station moved from the stock yard site to its present site off Park Road.

Returning now to the junction of Park Road and Main Street, turn left and follow the line of shops until you come upon the . . .

MECHANICS INSTITUTE (15)

The future of this unusual Main Street building is in doubt. Having served the town as library, school and town hall, its purpose for the future is unknown. In the year after its construction in 1864, the Institute was attended by over 350 members who could make use of a fine library of 6,000 volumes and a great variety of newspapers and periodicals. During the 1880's the committee commenced night classes in both arts and science, both of which were taken over by the Technical School in 1889. In 1926 the whole building was handed over to the town's library committee who recently

evacuated it for more palatial surroundings in the new shopping arcade.

There had been a Mechanics Institute in Bingley in 1832, but it soon disappeared. The textile workers of Wilsden managed to keep their institute going and built a solid 'home' for it in 1837. One of the members of that group, Thomas Wood, lived in Bingley. He and five others refounded the Mechanics Institute at Bingley in 1844, with small rooms and a library in Russell Street.

Twenty years later the present building was planned and built at a cost of £3,000. Local squirearchy avoided the subscription for they linked the association with radicalism and working-class politics. The premises provided, "a hall for lectures and music on the top floor, a reading room and class room on the ground floor and a spacious schoolroom for elementary instruction and other purposes in the basement". It became a great social centre for the working classes of Victorian Bingley.

Cross Main Street and make your way towards the dominating edifice of the Building Society! The road alongside leads to Myrtle Park, and to the rear of the swimming baths (Princess Hall) will be found . . .

MYRTLE GROVE (16)

For some years this building was the town hall, but it was originally erected in 1770 as a retreat for Johnson Atkinson Busfeild D.D., who had married Elizabeth Busfeild and taken her name at marriage in 1765. Inheriting several local estates by this marriage, J.A. Busfeild decided to erect a new country mansion on a farm site, formerly known as Spring Head. In April 1779 Wesley slept at the house and described the area

in his journal as "a little paradise". The house itself is only of two storeys, but its nine bay front and pedimented doorway are impressive. A mausoleum was planned in 1781 and although the ground was consecrated, it was never built.

J. A. Busfeild was elected as Registrar for the West Riding in 1809 and his son hoped that this might pay off some of his £45,000 of debts "the whole of your income from every source was many hundred pounds a year short of the annual interest of your debts . . . I might be able to keep you and myself out of prison". By that time Myrtle Park and the estate had passed into the hands of a Mr. Birch for £10,500. In 1810 the house was purchased by General Twiss of the Royal Engineers. He and his eight gardeners did much to alter the appearance of the grounds. Twiss died in 1827 and the estate was inherited by his son-in-law, Walker Ferrand of Harden Grange. The estate changed hands once more in 1874 when it was purchased by Alfred Sharp J.P. for £13,500.

The building came under municipal control in 1908 when it was relet into four separate dwellings, and the grounds were used as a second public park. Myrtle Grove officially became the Town Hall in 1926 when the interior of the building was changed drastically.

Overleaf: Myrtle Grove, formerly Bingley Town Hall.

Refer now to your map and cross the park and its famous Bottom Meadow, until you reach the bridge. Once over the River Aire you will come into Beckfoot Lane, an ancient highway through Airedale. Having reached the lane, turn right, and you will stumble upon the idyllic . . .

BECKFOOT BRIDGE & FARM (17)

This is one of the most picturesque spots of the whole area. Its rural simplicity and tranquility are, however, threatened by the modern planners' creation, the urban motorway. The bridge, which has a character all of its own, is a favourite with local and national artists. It stands upon the oldest road of the district; or what was probably the ancient forest road along the riverbank from Cottingley. It was certainly the old bridle and pack horse route from the lower Aire Valley to Bingley until the erection of a stone bridge over the river at Cottingley in the late 18th century. In 1723 the old wooden bridge at Beckfoot was replaced by the present stone bridge. Details of this can be seen in the Parish Book, and it was built by two local masons, Benjamin Craven and Joshua Scott at a cost of £10, and this included the price of maintenance for seven years.

Alongside the bridge stands Beckfoot Farm of equal antiquity. Over the doorway is a datestone marked 1617 ER IR AR. The lanterns on the corners of the farm show that the property was once owned by the Knights of St. John. Other inscriptions on the farm house reveal that the property once belonged to the Rawson family.

There was certainly a fulling mill at Beckfoot in the Elizabethan days, and shortly before the occupation of the Rawson

family in 1617, the farm was owned by Walter Morvill, a yeoman clothier. The probate inventory of the latter included the following:-

28 stones of wool	=	£21
Yarn & listings	=	£ 7 - 7 - 8
7 pieces of cloth	=	£13 - 10
Horse, saddle, wantow	=	£ 3 - 6 - 8
23 sheep	=	£ 4
Debts	=	£ 7 - 17
Credit	=	£26 - 16 - 10
A pair of lomes, healds and slaws	=	£1

On a main artery of the Aire valley transport system, Beckfoot was ideally placed for the farmer-clothier whose worsted trade functioned upon the 'putting out' system.

Cross the old pack-horse bridge and keep to the narrow lane. From Beckfoot Lane there is a fine view of Harden Grange, one of the many Ferrand family homes. The family first came to this site, with its lofty outlook over the whole valley in 1712. There is little left today of the original building. Reaching the end of Beckfoot Lane you will find yourself on the heavily gladed Harden Road, more colloquially, the Twines! Turn left towards Harden and you will soon reach the gateway to . . .

ST. IVES (& THE FERRANDS) (18)

In 1928 the Bingley Council purchased the vast St. Ives estate which lies north of the town across Ireland Bridge. The purchase included two fine buildings and about 800 acres of woodland and moorland. The estate had been in the possession of the Ferrand family since 1636, when Robert Ferrand bought the land.

Having acquired St. Ives, as his share of the Harden manor, Robert Ferrand built for himself a fine house, and from there practised his trades of clothier and gentleman farmer. The entrance to his residence bears the family coat of arms and the following inscription,

"If thou a house shalt finde
Built to thy mynde
And that without thy cost;
Serve thou the more
God and the poore,
And then my labour is not loste".

Written by George Herbert, the lines refer to the Ferrand advancement under the Clifford family. Weathering and erosion have made this inscription almost illegible. However, Robert Ferrand's son Benjamin spent most of his life in the former St. Ives (now known as Harden Grange). The present St. Ives stands alongside the Old Grange and today houses the Bingley Golf Club and the Sports Turf Research Institute.

This building lacks much of the character of the Grange which it overshadows. It has an uninteresting rectangular shape with an eastern frontage of almost two hundred feet. The name best associated with St. Ives is William Busfeild-Ferrand, whose memory is marked by a small obelisk, on the moor edge near Lady Blantyre's Rock. Busfeild-Ferrand was M.P. for Knaresborough and was a prominent member of the Ten-Hour Factory Reform movement. His political career was entirely devoted to that cause and also to the inadequacies of the 1834 Poor Law Amendment Act. In spite of this, he was

a typical member of the traditional English squirearchy and maintained the feudal relationship between lord and vassal with its condescending patronage on the one hand and respectful subservience on the other.

Perhaps the most impressive feature of St. Ives is the parkland which surrounds it. William Busfeild-Ferrand was responsible for this, planting pine trees and rhododendron bushes in 400 acres. The park surrounds a lake, fed by natural springs and beyond the parkland is a fine sweep of moorland. The flora and fauna of this whole area is so abundant that a Nature Trail has recently been devised.

The whole of St. Ives estate is well worth a visit and is a naturalist's paradise. For our purpose, follow Cross Gates Lane from the site of the mansion and journey towards Altar Road. Cross the road and continue in a straight line on the moorland with the Rough Rock escarpment to your left. A short walk, and you will be confronted with the impressive . . .

DRUID'S ALTAR (19)

This site stands amongst the great blocks of millstone grit, or rough rock, which are found north-west of the town, overlooking the Aire valley. Its prominent position certainly suggests that such a spot once saw the mystic practises of the ancient Brigantian race. This lofty, and often bleak, promontory was ideally suited to the Draconic worship of the Druid. Visited by Benjamin Disraeli in 1844, the site finds a place in his novel, "Sybil"

> "Some huge rocks, one of which, pre-eminent,
> above its fellows and having a broad flat head
> . . . was called Druid's Altar. The ground about

was strewn with stony fragments . . . the ruins of some ancient temple, . . . or relics of some ancient world".

Such conclusive evidence as this, has not been found around the great rocks, but flints, arrow-heads, ancient stone circles and unusual rock markings are in abundance on the surrounding moorlands. Other points which suggest the site as an ancient Druid temple include the elevated position, which faces the rising sun, and the once thick forest of oaks, which surrounded the whole area. The Druids, in fact, took their name from the Celtic word "derw" which means oak.

Local antiquarians have suggested that the cobbled way from the Brown Cow Inn to the Altar Lane is the ancient route of the Druids' sacrificial processions.

Returning to the town by way of Altar Road there are some panoramic views across the valley. It is a particularly advantageous point from which to see the Bailey Hills site. That vast open air museum of prehistoric cultures, Baildon Moor, dominates the skyline to the north-east. At the bottom of Altar Road on the Harden side of the river is the . . .

BROWN COW INN (20)

Situated on the opposite side of Ireland Bridge to the White Horse Inn and Old Main Street, this tavern site has served many more useful purposes than the sale of liquor. The actual building is of recent construction though its siting has not changed. For many years after 1753 the trustees of the Keighley-Bradford Turnpike Trust met at this hostelry to discuss the profits from tolls and the general running of the highway which they had created. In the same room, the local

Druid's Altar

The former Brown Cow Inn, Harden Road

magistracy functioned as the petty sessions and many a poor sinner made his way from the inn to the town's stocks, or to the County Gaol at York. When the local bench moved to more salubrious surroundings the room was taken by a former grammar school master who ran a small independent school, outside of the 1870 state system. Towards the end of the century the local board of health held its meetings at the Inn!!

However, the tavern is best known for its historical associations with the Chartist movement of the mid-19th century. This was a working-class movement designed to give greater political power to that class. The climax of its campaigns came in 1848 when the local Chartists drilled and manoeuvred on Harden Moor in preparation for the forthcoming revolution. Great moorland assemblies frightened local magistrates into summoning military assistance. On one occasion the Sunday service was interrupted when news reached the Parish Church that a great Chartist meeting was assembling on Harden Moor. The Church bells sounded the alarm and several hundred yeomanry marched up Altar Lane to find . . . an outdoor Primitive Methodist Camp meeting!

The riots finally broke out in May 1848 and sixteen local men were arrested. Two of the ringleaders were held in the upper room of the Brown Cow Inn, but a great crowd of workers stormed the tavern and smashed down its door. They made off with the prisoners over Ireland Bridge to the smithy where their shackles were removed. The taverns of the Brown Cow Inn and the White Horse Inn are spanned by . . .

IRELAND BRIDGE (21)

The road, or track, along the river from Cottingley and Beckfoot, is of great antiquity. The river had always been crossed at the bottom of Belbank Wood, or by the stepping stones opposite Ferrand Lane, a fording of the river since prehistoric times.

Throughout the middle-ages the wooden bridge had been used by pedestrians and horses, but not carts. Its maintenance and repair were part of the Constable's annual assessment. However, in 1683 the bridge was in a serious state of neglect, and heavy trading traffic was increasing.

As it was an ancient Riding bridge, the magistrates at the Quarter Sessions of April 1686 decided to advance £270 for the construction of a stone bridge which had been estimated at £450. This was done, although it was considerably widened a century later. However, the major stonework and foundation of the bridge remains that of the 17th century structure.

Why Ireland Bridge? There are several theories, most of them based upon the gossip which was heard upon the bridge itself, for in the 19th century it was a popular gathering place for the gossips of the town. However, it may refer to Bailey Hills position as an island, or to the parallel of the Irish Sea, for it divides two very separate and rival manors.

The Bingley History trail has now reached the original point of departure, Old Main Street. I hope this little booklet has thrown new light, or provided new dimensions, to sites and buildings that are so often taken for granted. I have earnestly endeavoured to make sure all the facts are correct. I accept full responsibility for any inaccuracies, in the sincere hope that there are none.

* * *

William Shaw ... rv.t sober laborious & faithfull who at 2.s per Week for above 40 Years in one family maintaind a Wife & numerous Essue Dyed Dec: 14 Anno S Ætat: 78 Dom: 1726